Basic English Grammar for Kids

 1

JN104751

Complete the maze from **A** to **Z**. （下のA〜Zまで進んでゴールをめざそう）

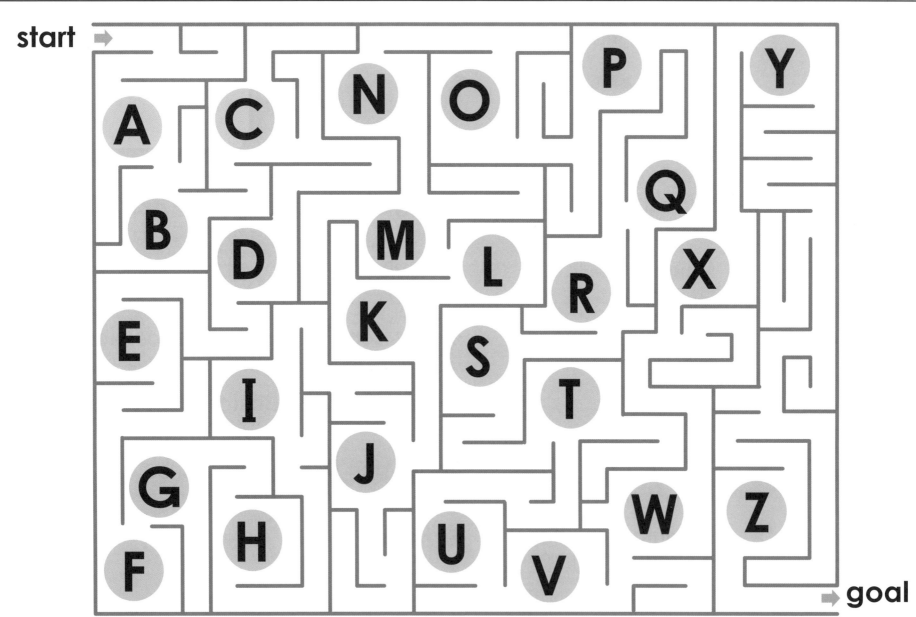

Complete the maze from **a** to **z**.　（下の**a**～**z**まで進んでゴールをめざそう）

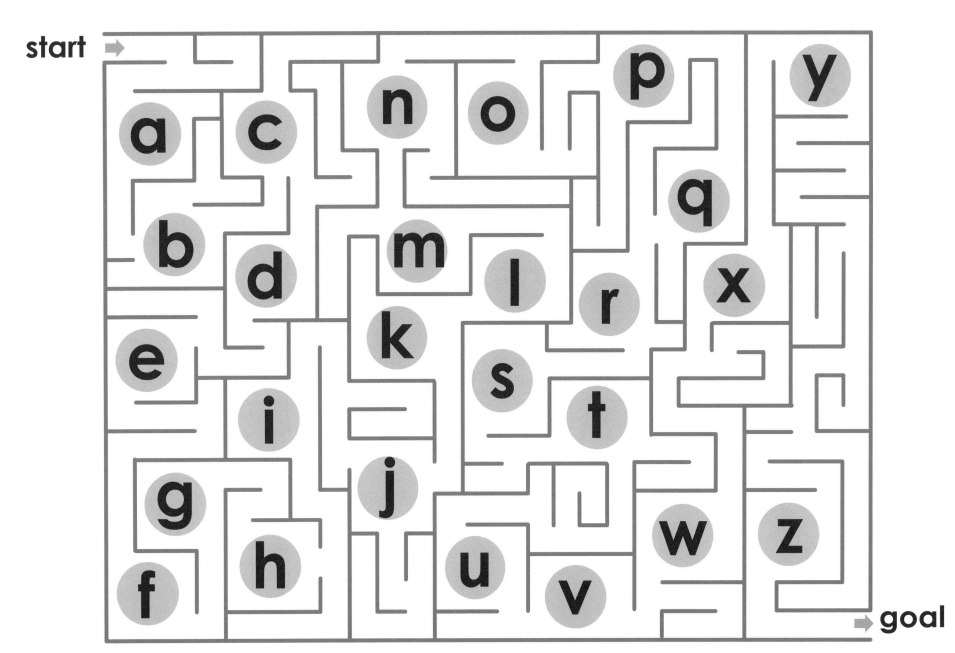

start

goal

Let's trace the letters! （アルファベットの大文字をなぞろう！）

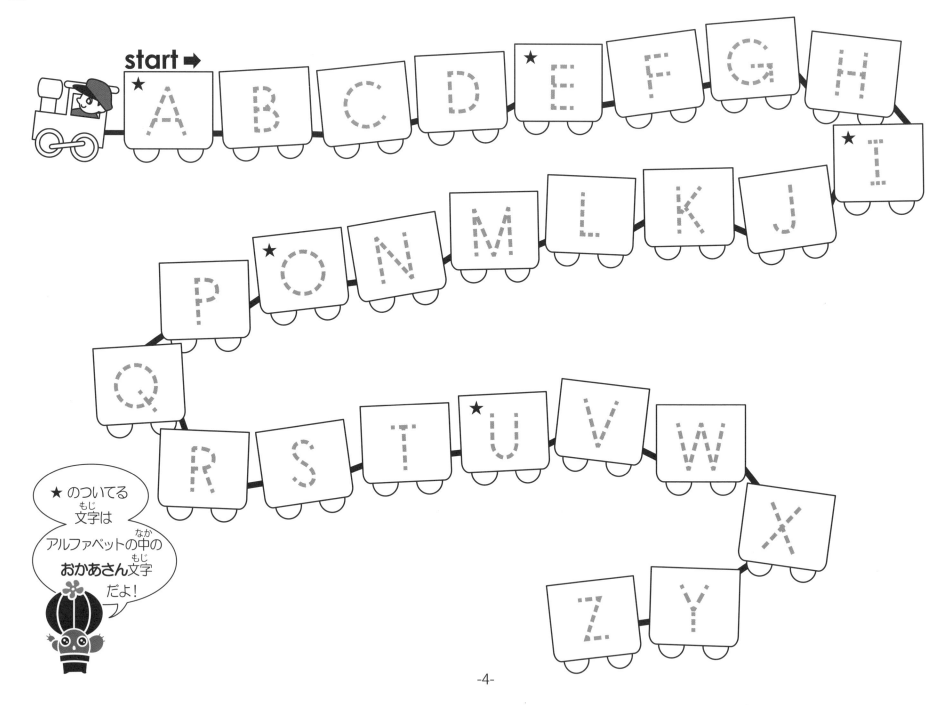

-4-

Let's trace the letters! （アルファベットの小文字をなぞろう！）

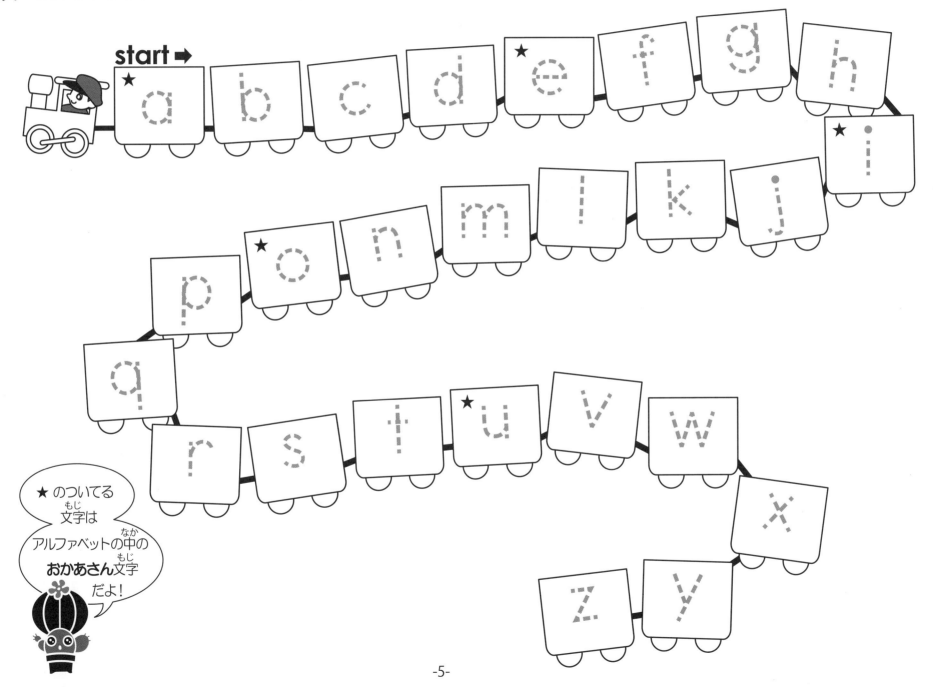

★ のついてる
文字は
アルファベットの中の
おかあさん文字
だよ！

-5-

Match the lowercase letters to the uppercase letters. （小文字に合う大文字を線で結ぼう）

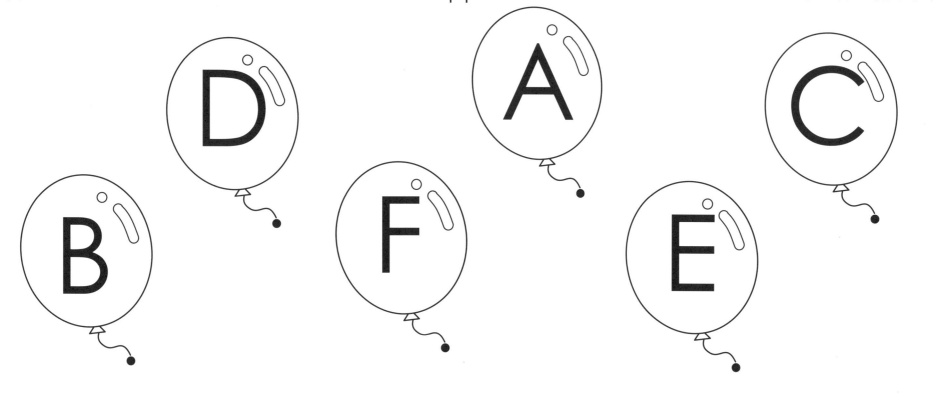

    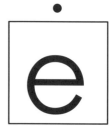

Match the lowercase letters to the uppercase letters. （小文字に合う大文字を線で結ぼう）

 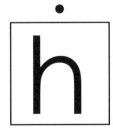  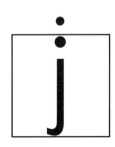 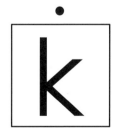 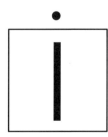

Match the lowercase letters to the uppercase letters.（小文字に合う大文字を線で結ぼう）

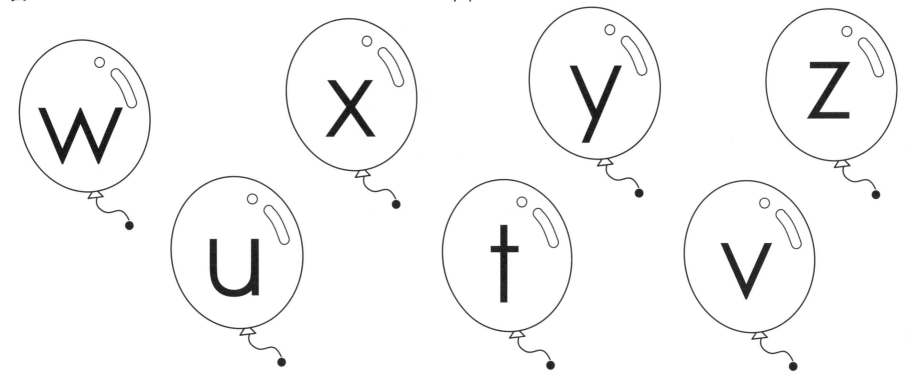

アルファベット26文字の中で下の5つの文字はお母さん文字（母音）だよ。すごく大切だから覚えてね。

 大文字

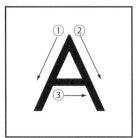 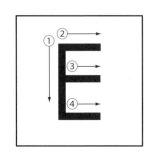 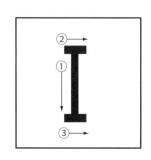 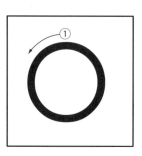 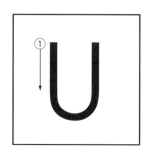

Write the letters on the dotted lines. （点線の上に文字を書こう）

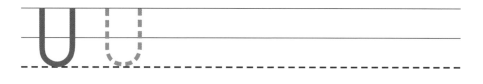

とっても働きものだよ！
しっかり覚えてね！！

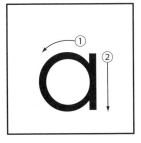  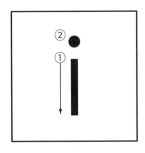 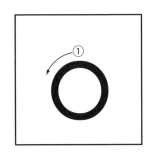 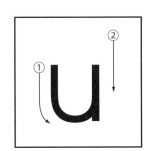

Write the letters on the dotted lines. （点線の上に文字を書こう）

a a

e e

i i

o o

u u

覚えるヒント
『ア』『イ』『ウ』『エ』『オ』とも
読めるよ！

Circle the vowels below. （お母さん文字（母音）を見つけて全部〇をつけよう）

P H E X K

G A I O T

S U F Q Z

5つ
みつけられたかな？

Circle the vowels below. （お母さん文字（母音）を見つけて全部 ◯ をつけよう）

Y D O N S B X

T Q V E P C M

I L K U Z F A

5つ
みつけられたかな？

-13-

y d o n s b x

t q v e p c m

i l k u z f a

5つ
みつけられたかな？

Circle the vowels below.

（お母さん文字（母音）を見つけて全部 ◯ をつけよう）

 ヒント！
a e i o u

全部で **10** こ見つけた？

m a p

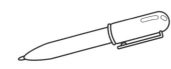

p e n

f o x

h a t

k e y

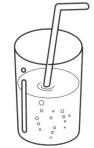

j u i c e

r o c k e t

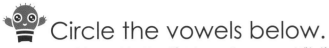 Circle the vowels below.

（お母さん文字（母音）を見つけて全部 ◯ をつけよう）

ヒント！

| a | e | i | o | u |

全部で 10 こ見つけた？

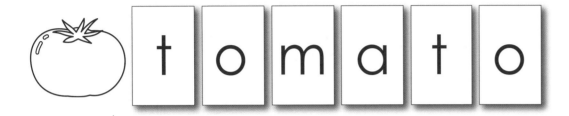

t o m a t o

f i r e

n u r s e

p e n g u i n

Write the first letter of the word. （言葉の最初の文字を書いてみよう）

 ヒント！
a e i o u

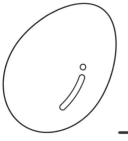 __gg

__ven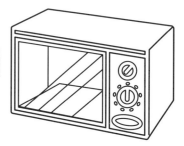

 __mbrella

 __pple

 __guana

Write the first letter of the word. <ruby>言葉<rt>ことば</rt></ruby>の<ruby>最初<rt>さいしょ</rt></ruby>の<ruby>文字<rt>もじ</rt></ruby>を<ruby>書<rt>か</rt></ruby>いてみよう

ヒント！

a e i o u

___lligator

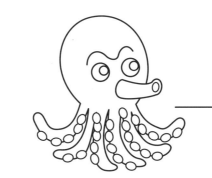
___ctopus

___ce cream

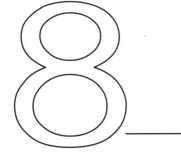
___ight

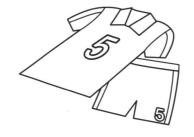
___niform

Section 3 | **Basic Sentences** (英語で文を作ろう！)

Write the missing letter for each sentence.

(小文字を1字入れて文を完成させよう)

ヒント！

| l / e / a / c |

のどれかが入るよ！

①  It is an ___nt.

②  It is a ___at.

③ 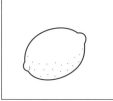 It is a ___emon.

言葉の前につく

『a』と『an』。

いったい
どんな意味？
答えは28ページ
を見てね！

④ 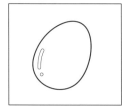 It is an ___gg.

-20-

Write the missing letter for each sentence.
（小文字を1字入れて文を完成させよう）

ヒント！

o / s / f / m

のどれかが入るよ！

①  It is a ___rog.

②  It is a ___ouse.

③  It is a ___trawberry.

言葉の前につく

『a』と『an』。

いったい
どんな意味？
答えは28ページ
を見てね！

④  It is an ___ctopus.

Write the missing letter for each sentence.

（小文字を1字入れて文を完成させよう）

ヒント！

b / y / t / k

のどれかが入るよ！

①  It is a ___all.

②  It is a ___ey.

③  It is a ___o-yo.

④  It is a ___ree.

言葉の前につく

『a』と『an』。

いったい
どんな意味？
答えは28ページ
を見てね！

Write the missing letter for each sentence.

（小文字を1字入れて文を完成させよう）

ヒント！

z / q / c / u

のどれかが入るよ！

①  It is a ___ow.

② It is a ___ebra.

③ It is a ___ueen.

④  It is an ___mbrella.

言葉の前につく

『a』と『an』。

いったい
どんな意味？

答えは28ページ
を見てね！

Write the missing letter for each sentence.

（小文字を1字入れて文を完成させよう）

ヒント！

n / w / d / p / r

のどれかが入るよ！

①  It is a ___ig.

②  It is a ___abbit.

③  It is a ___et.

④  It is a ___og.

⑤ 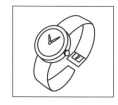 It is a ___atch.

言葉の前につく

『a』と『an』。

いったい
どんな意味？
答えは28ページ
を見てね！

Write the missing letter for each sentence.

（小文字を1字入れて文を完成させよう）

ヒント！

g / h / i / v / x

のどれかが入るよ！

①  It is a ___orilla.

②  It is an ___ce cream.

③  It is a ___iolin.

④  It is a ___at.

⑤ 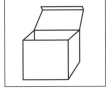 It is a bo___.

言葉の前につく

『a』と『an』。

いったい
どんな意味？
答えは28ページ
を見てね！

-25-

Write the names on the lines. (線の上に名前を書こう)

名前は
さいしょの文字が
大文字になるよ！

① My name is E r i n .
What's your name?

My name is [ ]_____.

② What's your mother's name?

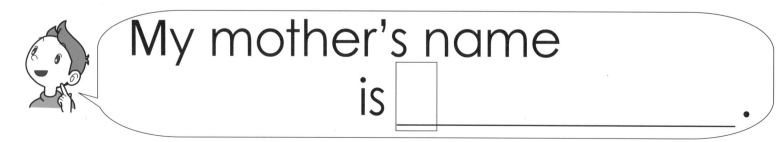

My mother's name
is [ ]_____.

Write the missing letter for each conversation. （小文字を1字入れて文を完成させよう）

①  What is it?

  It is a __tomato.

②  What is it?

  It is an __gg.

③  What is it?

  It is a __umpkin.

④  What is it?

  It is an __nion.

Section 4 "a" vs "an" (a / an ってなあに？)

 Read the sentences. (下の文を読んでみよう)

① It is a cake.　　　　　　（それは1コのケーキです）

② It is an orange.　　　　　（それは1コのオレンジです）

③ It is a lion.　　　　　　　（それは1頭のライオンです）

④ It is an umbrella.　　　　（それは1本のかさです）

⑤ It is a book.　　　　　　　（それは1さつの本です）

 スペシャル問題！！　a / anは、どんな意味のことば？　□に数字を入れてね。

a / anは、□つということ。

 Read the sentences. (下の文を読んでみよう)

① It is (~~a~~ / (an)) apple.

② It is (~~a~~ / (an)) egg.

③ It is (~~a~~ / (an)) ice cream.

④ It is (~~a~~ / (an)) octopus.

⑤ It is (~~a~~ / (an)) umbrella.

スペシャル問題!!

『a』を『an』に変身させる5つの文字を□に書いてみよう!

『a』は上の5つの文字の前にくると『an』に変身するよ。

 Circle "a" or "an."　（『a』か『an』を選んで ◯ をつけよう）

① 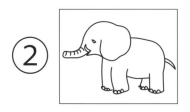 It is (a / an) <u>c</u>ar.

② 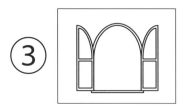 It is (a / an) <u>e</u>lephant.

③ It is (a / an) <u>w</u>indow.

④  It is (a / an) <u>p</u>enguin.

⑤ 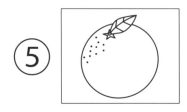 It is (a / an) <u>o</u>range.

-30-

いちばん最初の文字を
よく見てね！

① 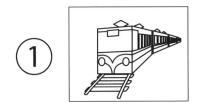 It is (a / an) <u>t</u>rain.

② 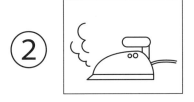 It is (a / an) <u>i</u>ron.

③  It is (a / an) <u>b</u>ook.

④  It is (a / an) <u>k</u>angaroo.

⑤ 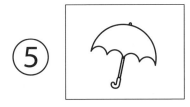 It is (a / an) <u>u</u>mbrella.

 Write "a" and "an." （『a』と『an』を書いてみよう）

 Write "a" or "an." （『a』か『an』を書いてみよう）

①  It is ＿＿＿ <u>a</u>pron.

② It is ＿＿＿ <u>t</u>urtle.

③ It is ＿＿＿ <u>p</u>umpkin.

④ It is ＿＿＿ <u>u</u>mbrella.

ヒント！
いちばん最初の文字を
よく見てね！

 Write "a" or "an."　　『a』か『an』を書いてみよう

① It is _____ <u>s</u>nake.

② It is _____ <u>i</u>gloo.

③ It is _____ <u>e</u>ggplant.

④ It is _____ <u>h</u>orse.

⑤ It is _____ <u>o</u>nion.

ヒント！
いちばん最初の文字を
よく見てね！

【例】

It is a panda.

①

It is ☐ alligator.

②

It is ☐ lion.

③

It is ☐ elephant.

④

It is ☐ gorilla.

 ちゃんと言えるかな?

5 It is ☐ iguana.

6  It is ☐ owl.

7  It is ☐ rabbit.

8  It is ☐ fox.

9  It is ☐ koala.

Say it! Write "a" or "an" and read the sentences. (『a』か『an』を書いて文を読んでみよう)

【例】

It is ☐ a ☐ jellyfish.

①

It is ☐ ☐ dolphin.

②

It is ☐ ☐ octopus.

③

It is ☐ ☐ crab.

ちゃんと言えるかな？

④

It is ☐ ☐ penguin.

⑤  It is [ ] eel.

⑥  It is [ ] starfish.

⑦ It is [ ] ray.

⑧  It is [ ] turtle.

⑨  It is [ ] orca.

Say it! Write "a" or "an" and read the sentences. (『a』か『an』を書いて文を読んでみよう)

【例】

It is | a | boat.

①

It is | | bus.

②

It is | | train.

③

It is | | helicopter.

④

It is | | ambulance.

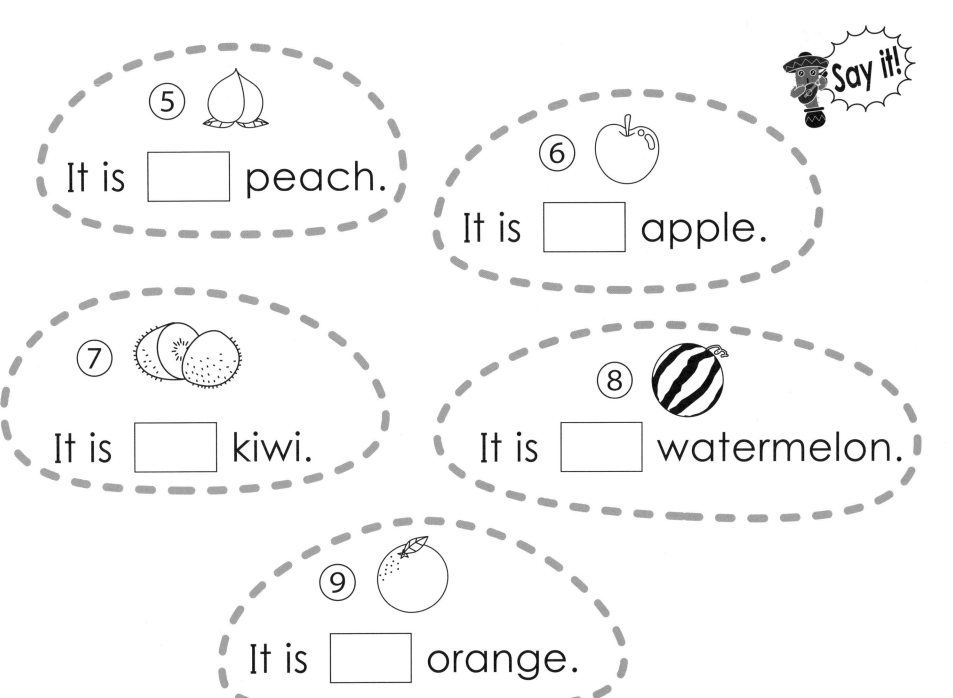

⑤ It is ☐ peach.

⑥ It is ☐ apple.

⑦ It is ☐ kiwi.

⑧ It is ☐ watermelon.

⑨ It is ☐ orange.

【例】

⇨ It is an apple.

（それは1コのりんごです）

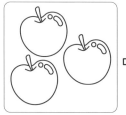

⇨ They are apples.

（それらはいくつかのりんごです）

下の文を読んでみよう。

⇨ It is a ball.

（それは1つのボールです）

⇨ They are balls.

（それらはいくつかのボールです）

クイズ

『a』と『an』がつく時と
最後に『s』がつく時では
何がちがうかな？

 ⟹ It is __ hat.

（それは1つのぼうしです）

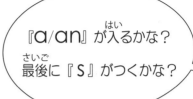 『a/an』が入るかな？
最後に『S』がつくかな？

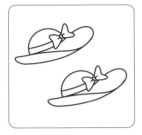 ⟹ They are hat__.

（それらはいくつかのぼうしです）

 ⟹ It is __ violin.

（それは1つのヴァイオリンです）

 ⟹ They are violin__.

（それらはいくつかのヴァイオリンです）

Match the picture to the correct sentence. (絵に合った文を選んで線で結ぼう)

①  •

- It is **an** umbrella.

- They are umbrella**s**.

② 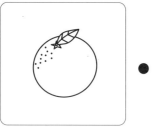 •

- It is **an** orange.

- They are orange**s**.

③  •

- It is **an** elephant.

- They are elephant**s**.

④

- It is **an** owl.
- They are owl**s**.

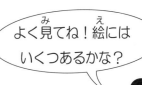

よく見てね！絵には いくつあるかな？

⑤

- It is **a** tree.
- They are tree**s**.

⑥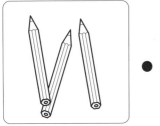

- It is **a** pencil.
- They are pencil**s**.

 **Say it!** Match the sentences to the correct pictures.
（文に合った絵を選んで線で結ぼう）

① They are <u>kite<mark>s</mark></u>.　•

•　

② It is <mark>a</mark> <u>horse</u>.　•

•　

③ It is <mark>a</mark> <u>whale</u>.　•

•　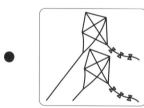

④ They are <u>flower<mark>s</mark></u>. •

•　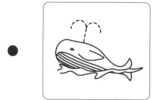

⑤ It is <mark>an</mark> <u>igloo</u>.　•

•　

Say it! Match the sentences to the correct pictures.
（文に合った絵を選んで線で結ぼう）

① They are lions.   •

② They are eggs.   •

③ It is an ant.   •

④ They are dogs.   •

⑤ It is a star.   •

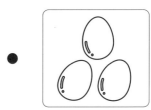

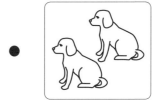

Make a circle in the □ of each "he" picture below.

（『he(かれ)』の絵を選んで□に◯をつけよう）

①

②

③

④

⑤

⑥

 Trace the words and read the sentences. Then write the number of the correct pictures. （点線をなぞってから文を読んでみよう。文に合う絵を選びその番号を書こう）

① He is a boy.　　　（　　　）番の絵

② He is a doctor.　（　　　）番の絵

Make a circle in the □ of each "he" picture below.

『he(かれ)』の絵を選んで□に◯をつけよう

Trace the words and read the sentences. Then write the number of the correct pictures. （点線をなぞってから文を読んでみよう。文に合う絵を選びその番号を書こう）

① He is a teacher. （　　）番の絵

② He is a police officer. （　　）番の絵

③ He is a pilot. （　　）番の絵

Make a circle in the □ of each "she" picture below.

（『she（かのじょ）』の絵を選んで□に◯をつけよう）

①

②

③

④

⑤

⑥

 Trace the words and read the sentences. Then write the number of the correct pictures. （点線をなぞってから文を読んでみよう。文に合う絵を選びその番号を書こう）

① She is a student. （　　　）番の絵

② She is a nurse. （　　　）番の絵

Make a circle in the □ of each "she" picture below.

『she(かのじょ)』の絵を選んで□に◯をつけよう)

Trace the words and read the sentences. Then write the number of the correct pictures. (点線をなぞってから文を読んでみよう。文に合う絵を選びその番号を書こう)

① She is a dancer. (　　)番の絵

② She is a queen. (　　)番の絵

③ She is a farmer. (　　)番の絵

Make a circle in the □ of each "it" picture below.
(『it (それ)』の絵を選んで □ に ◯ をつけよう)

① 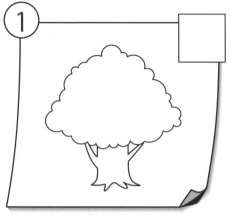 □

②  □

③  □

④ 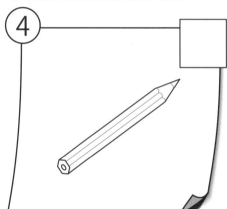 □

⑤  □

⑥  □

 Trace the words and read the sentences. Then write the number of the correct pictures. (点線をなぞってから文を読んでみよう。文に合う絵を選びその番号を書こう)

① It is a horse. (　　)番の絵

② It is a tree. (　　)番の絵

Make a circle in the □ of each "it" picture below.(『it（それ）』の絵を選んで □ に ◯ をつけよう)

Trace the words and read the sentences. Then write the number of the correct pictures.　(点線をなぞってから文を読んでみよう。文に合う絵を選びその番号を書こう)

① It is an apple.　　　（　　　）番の絵

② It is a chair.　　　（　　　）番の絵

③ It is a cat.　　　（　　　）番の絵

Make a circle in the □ of each "they" picture below.

（『they（かれら/かのじょたち/それら）』の絵を選んで□に◯をつけよう）

①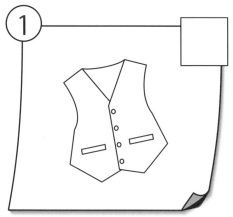

②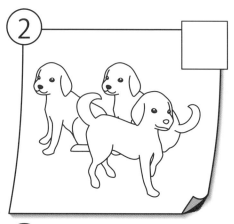

③

④

⑤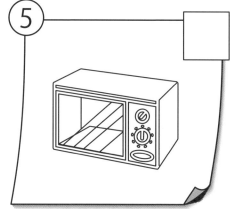

⑥

 Trace the words and read the sentences. Then write the number of the correct pictures.　（点線をなぞってから文を読んでみよう。文に合う絵を選びその番号を書こう）

① They are girls.　（　　）番の絵

② They are dogs.　（　　）番の絵

-54-

Make a circle in the □ of each "they" picture below.
(『they (かれら/かのじょたち/それら)』の絵を選んで□に ◯ をつけよう)

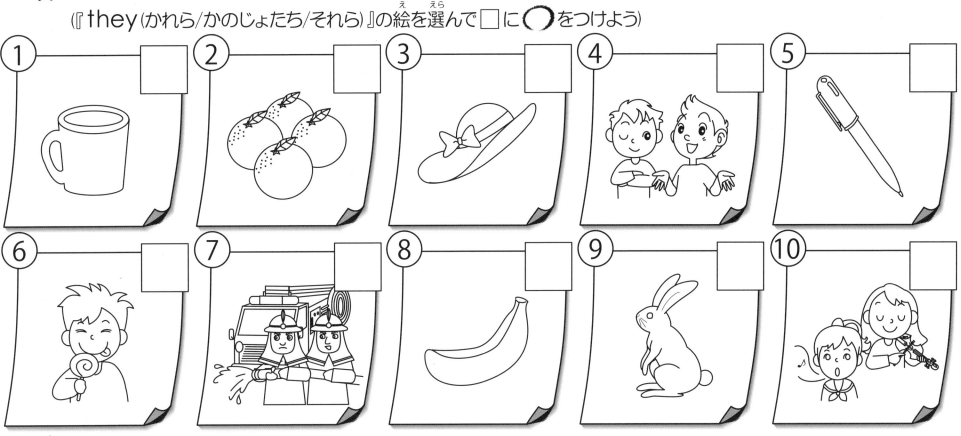

Trace the words and read the sentences. Then write the number of the correct pictures. (点線をなぞってから文を読んでみよう。文に合う絵を選びその番号を書こう)

① They are boys. ( ) 番の絵

② They are firefighters. ( ) 番の絵

③ They are oranges. ( ) 番の絵

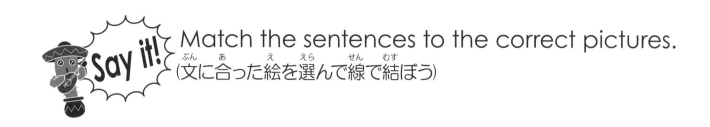 Match the sentences to the correct pictures.
（文に合った絵を選んで線で結ぼう）

① <u>He</u> is a boy. •

② <u>They</u> are pandas. •

③ <u>She</u> is a grandmother. •

④ <u>It</u> is an umbrella. •

⑤ <u>They</u> are pencils. •

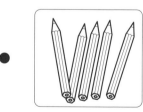

 Match the sentences to the correct pictures.

 (文に合った絵を選んで線で結ぼう)

① <u>She</u> is a queen.   •

② <u>It</u> is a watch.   •

③ <u>They</u> are pigs.   •

④ <u>He</u> is a king.   •

⑤ <u>They</u> are girls.   •

Say it! Write the correct word to complete each sentence.
（右の枠の中から言葉を選んで書き文を完成しよう。）

①  _____ is a student.

ここから
選んでネ！
↓

②  _____ is an umbrella.

③  _____ are pandas.

④  _____ is a dentist.

⑤  _____ are boys.

He

She

It

They

 **Say it!** Write the correct word to complete each sentence.

（右の枠の中から言葉を選んで書き文を完成しよう。）

① 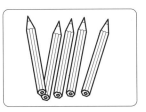 _____ are pencils.

②  _____ are grapes.

③  _____ is a horse.

④  _____ is a firefighter.

⑤  _____ is a nurse.

 ここから選んでネ！

He

She

It

They

-59-

Challenge — Let's practice using "he," "she," "it" and "they."
『he』『she』『it』『they』を使って言ってみよう!

① 【例】 <u>He</u> is a teacher.

② _____ is an apple.

③ _____ are pencils.

④ _____ is a student.

⑤ _____ is a boy.

Write the correct Japanese on the lines.
(「うさぎ」はどこにいる?日本語の線のところに「うさぎ」のいる"ばしょ"を書いてみよう)

 ⇒ It is │ on │ the hat.

うさぎはどこにいる?　⇒　ぼうしの＿＿＿＿にいます。

 ⇒ It is │ in │ the hat.

うさぎはどこにいる?　⇒　ぼうしの＿＿＿＿にいます。

 ⇒ It is │ under │ the hat.

うさぎはどこにいる?　⇒　ぼうしの＿＿＿＿にいます。

on➡上 / in➡中 / under➡下 ということ。

Where's the apple? Let's practice writing the words.
（絵を見て「りんご」はどこにあるかな？　書く練習もしようね）

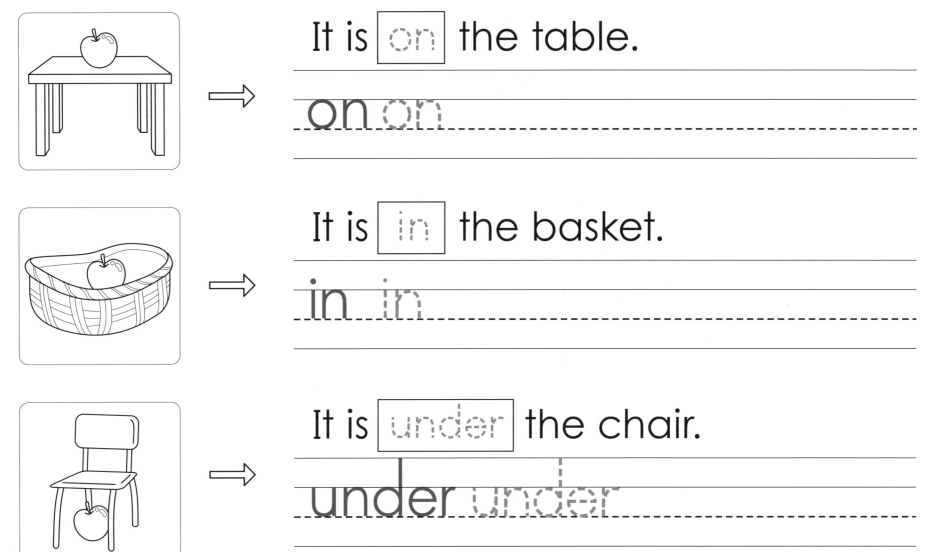

It is │ on │ the table.

on on

It is │ in │ the basket.

in in

It is │ under │ the chair.

under under

Read the sentences and draw a ball in each picture.
（文を読んでボールを絵の中に描いてみよう）

① A ball is │under│ the table. ⇒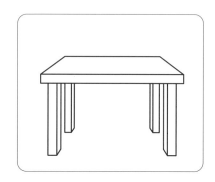

② A ball is │on│ the bed. ⇒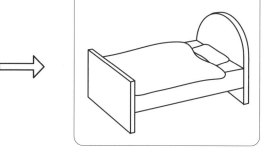

③ A ball is │in│ the basket.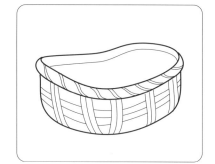

Read the sentences and draw an apple in each picture.
（文を読んでボールを絵の中に描いてみよう）

① An apple is on the table. ⇒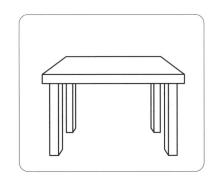

② An apple is in the basket. ⇒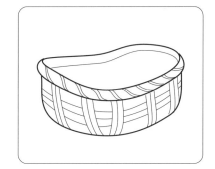

③ An apple is under the tree. ⇒

Where are they? Look at the pictures and circle the correct word.

（「りんご」や「動物」はどこにいるかな？　絵を見て一番合う言葉を選び〇をつけてね)

①  They are (on / in / under) the tree.

②  It is (on / in / under) the cage.

③  They are (on / in / under) the basket.

Where are they? Look at the pictures and circle the correct word.

（「りんご」や「動物」はどこにいるかな？　絵を見て一番合う言葉を選び ◯ をつけてね）

①  It is $\left(\begin{array}{c}\text{on}\\\text{in}\\\text{under}\end{array}\right)$ the hat.

②  They are $\left(\begin{array}{c}\text{on}\\\text{in}\\\text{under}\end{array}\right)$ the plate.

③  It is $\left(\begin{array}{c}\text{on}\\\text{in}\\\text{under}\end{array}\right)$ the chair.

Say it! Look at the pictures. Choose the correct word for each picture from the ⬜ and write it on the line. Then read the sentences.

絵を見て、それが「どこ」にあるか ⬜ から選び線の上に書いてみよう！ それから英文を読んでみよう！

Where is the cat? （そのネコはどこにいるの？）

on
in
under

 ⟹ It is _____ the box.

 ⟹ It is _____ the bed.

 ⟹ It is _____ the table.

Say it! Look at the pictures. Choose the correct word for each picture from the ⬜ and write it on the line. Then read the sentences.

絵を見て、それが「どこ」にあるか ⬜ から選び線の上に書いてみよう！ それから英文を読んでみよう！

Where are the balls? （そのボールはどこにあるの？）

on	
in	
under	

 ⟹ They are _____ the slide.

 ⟹ They are _____ the bed.

 ⟹ They are _____ the box.

Look at the pictures. Choose the correct word for each picture from the ☐ and write it on the line. Then read the sentences.

絵を見て、それが「どこ」にあるか ☐ から選び線の上に書いてみよう！ それから英文を読んでみよう！

| on |
| in |
| under |

①

Where is the ball?

It is _____ the box.

②

Where are the cats?

They are _____ the bed.

③

Where is the apple?

It is _____ the table.

『where』は"ばしょ"を聞くときに使う言葉で"どこ？"だよ！

Say it! Look at the pictures. Choose the correct word for each picture from the ⬜ and write it on the line. Then read the sentences.

絵を見て、それが「どこ」にあるか ⬜ から選び線の上に書いてみよう！ それから英文を読んでみよう！

① Where are the balls?

They are _____ the slide.

---

② Where is the cat?

It is _____ the table.

---

③ Where are the apples?

They are _____ the bowl.

on
in
under

『where』は
"ばしょ"を聞くときに
使う言葉で
"どこ?"だよ!

-71-

Say it! Let's practice using "on," "in " and "under."
(『on』『in』『under』を使って言ってみよう)

① どこにいるの？
【例】 It is <u>in</u> the box.

② どこにいるの？
It is ___ the jungle gym.

③ どこにいるの？
It is ___ the tree.

④ どこにいるの？
They are ___ the slide.

Section 8 Basic Adjectives （人や物の "ようす" を表すことば）

The words in the ▦ are adjectives. Write the adjectives in Japanese.

▦ のある英語は人や物の"ようす"を表すことばだよ。どんな"ようす"なのか □ の中に日本語で書いてみよう！

It is big.

それ（うさぎ）は □ です。

It is small.

それ（うさぎ）は □ です。

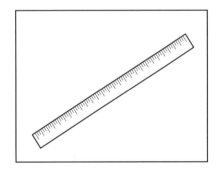

It is long.

それ（じょうぎ）は □ です。

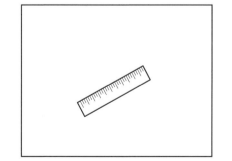

It is short.

それ（じょうぎ）は □ です。

The words in the ▢ are adjectives. Write the adjectives in Japanese.

▢のある英語は人や物の"ようす"を表すことばだよ。どんな"ようす"なのか▢の中に日本語で書いてみよう！

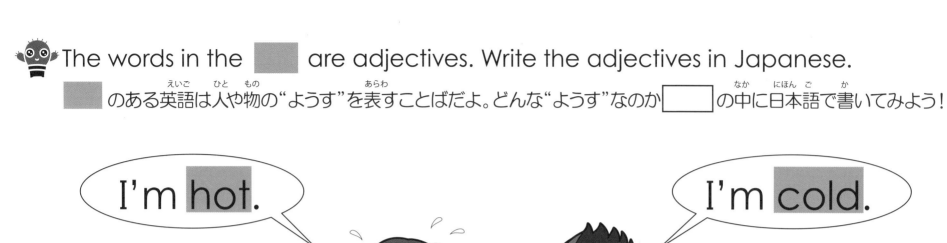

I'm hot.

わたしは ▢ いです。

I'm cold.

ぼくは ▢ いです。

I'm hungry.

ぼくは おなかが ▢ 。

I'm full.

わたしは おなかが ▢ 。

Circle the correct adjective for each picture.

（絵を見てみよう！ 絵の"ようす"に当てはまる方に ◯ をつけよう！）

① 　They are $\left(\begin{array}{c}\text{hot}\\\text{cold}\end{array}\right)$.

② 　They are $\left(\begin{array}{c}\text{full}\\\text{hungry}\end{array}\right)$.

③ 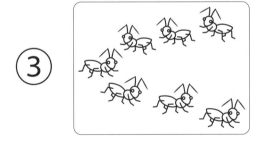　They are $\left(\begin{array}{c}\text{big}\\\text{small}\end{array}\right)$.

④ 　They are $\left(\begin{array}{c}\text{long}\\\text{short}\end{array}\right)$.

（絵を見てみよう！　絵の"ようす"に当てはまる方に ◯ をつけよう！）

①  It is $\left(\begin{array}{c}\text{big}\\\text{small}\end{array}\right)$.

②  It is $\left(\begin{array}{c}\text{long}\\\text{short}\end{array}\right)$.

③  He is $\left(\begin{array}{c}\text{hot}\\\text{cold}\end{array}\right)$.

④  She is $\left(\begin{array}{c}\text{full}\\\text{hungry}\end{array}\right)$.

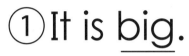 **Say it!** Match the sentences to the correct pictures.
(文に合った絵を選んで線で結ぼう)

① It is <u>big</u>.　　　　　●

② He is <u>hungry</u>.　　　●

③ They are <u>short</u>.　　●

④ It is <u>small</u>.　　　　●

⑤ She is <u>full</u>.　　　　●

 Say it! Match the sentences to the correct pictures.
（文に合った絵を選んで線で結ぼう）

① It is <u>long</u>. • •

② They are <u>big</u>. • •

③ She is <u>hot</u>. • •

④ They are <u>small</u>. • •

⑤ He is <u>cold</u>. • •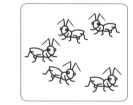

Say it! Which adjective is it? Let's practice speaking.
（どんなようすなのかな？　言ってみよう！）

① 【例】 He is <u>cold</u>.

② She is _____.

③ He is _____.

④ She is _____.

⑤ It is _____.

Section 9 | Basic Verbs （"うごき" を表すことば）

Look at the underlined words. They are called "verbs." Let's read.
（下の線のことばは"うごき"を表すことばだよ。読んでみよう）

I <u>open</u> the box.

I <u>close</u> the curtains.

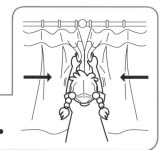

I <u>sit</u> down.

I <u>stand</u> up.

Trace the verbs below. Then match the sentences to the correct pictures.
（次の英文の点線のことばをなぞってから、あてはまる絵と線でむすぼう）

① I open the box. •   •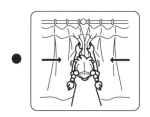

② I close the curtains. •   •

③ I sit down. •   •

④ I stand up. •   •

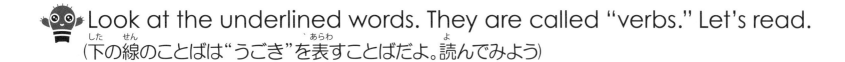 Look at the underlined words. They are called "verbs." Let's read.
（下の線のことばは"うごき"を表すことばだよ。読んでみよう）

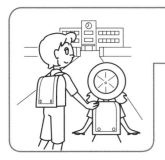 I <u>go</u> to school.

I <u>swim</u> in the sea.

 I <u>walk</u> to the house.

I <u>run</u> in the park.

Trace the verbs below. Then match the sentences to the correct pictures.
(次の英文の点線のことばをなぞってから、あてはまる絵と線でむすぼう)

① I go to school. •   •

② I swim in the sea. •   •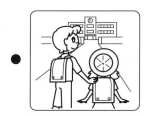

③ I run in the park. •   •

④ I walk to the house. •   •

 Look at the underlined words. They are called "verbs." Let's read.

（下の線のことばは"うごき"を表すことばだよ。読んでみよう）

 I catch a ball.

I throw a ball.

 I pull the dog.

I push the button.

Trace the verbs below. Then match the sentences to the correct pictures.

(次の英文の点線のことばをなぞってから、あてはまる絵と線でむすぼう)

① I pull the dog. •

② I push the button. •

③ I catch a ball. •

④ I throw a ball. •

 Look at the underlined words. They are called "verbs." Let's read.
（下の線のことばは"うごき"を表すことばだよ。読んでみよう）

 I <u>cook</u> lunch.

I <u>eat</u> curry.

 I <u>drink</u> water.

I <u>cut</u> the paper.

 I <u>sing</u> in the room.

I <u>sleep</u> in the bed.

Trace the verbs below. Then match the sentences to the correct pictures.

（次の英文の点線のことばをなぞってから、あてはまる絵と線でむすぼう）

① I cut the paper.   •   •

② I eat curry.   •   •

③ I sing in the room.   •   •

④ I cook lunch.   •   •

⑤ I drink water.   •   •

⑥ I sleep in the bed.   •   •

 **Say it!** Look at the sentences. Write the number of the verb for each picture on the lines.

（次の英文の＿＿に合うことばを 〔　　　〕 から選んで番号を入れ、完成した文を読んでみよう！）

(1) push

(2) sleep

(3) drink

(4) throw

  I ___ the button.

I ___ water.

 I ___ in the bed.

  I ___ a ball.

 **Say it!** Look at the sentences. Write the number of the verb for each picture on the lines.

（次の英文の＿＿に合うことばを ▨ から選んで番号を入れ、完成した文を読んでみよう！）

(1) run

(2) go

(3) cut

(4) eat

①  I ___ the paper.

②  I ___ in the park.

③  I ___ curry.

④ 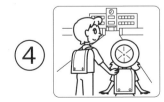 I ___ to school.

 **Say it!** Look at the sentences. Write the number of the verb for each picture on the lines.

（次の英文の＿＿に合うことばを 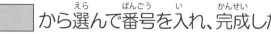 から選んで番号を入れ、完成した文を読んでみよう！）

(1) sit
(2) pull
(3) close
(4) catch

①  I ＿＿ the dog.

②  I ＿＿ down.

③  I ＿＿ a ball.

④ 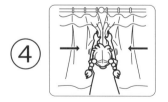 I ＿＿ the curtains.

 スペシャル問題！！ Read each sentence and check the ☐.
（文を読んで☐にチェックをしよう！）

① Please **open** the window. ☐

② Please **run** in the park. ☐

③ Please **pull** the door. ☐

④ Please **sing** a song. ☐

⑤ Please **cook** lunch. ☐

スペシャル問題！！ Read each sentence and check the ☐.
（文を読んで☐にチェックをしよう！）

① Please sit down. ☐

② Please throw the ball. ☐

③ Please cut the paper. ☐

④ Please catch the eraser. ☐

⑤ Please close the curtains. ☐

スペシャル問題!! Read each sentence and check the ☐.
（文を読んで☐にチェックをしよう！）

① Please drink water. ☐

② Please push the door. ☐

③ Please eat lunch. ☐

④ Please walk to the wall. ☐

⑤ Please sleep. ☐

⑥ Please stand up. ☐

Vocabulary List

Noun

a	alligator	**d**	dancer		horse		onion		slide
	ambulance		dentist		house		orange		snake
	ant		doctor	**i**	ice cream		orca		song
	apple		dog		igloo		oven		star
	apron		dolphin		iguana		owl		starfish
b	ball		door		iron	**p**	panda		strawberry
	basket	**e**	eel	**j**	jellyfish		paper		student
	bed		egg		juice		park	**t**	table
	boat		eggplant		jungle gym		peach		teacher
	book		eight	**k**	kangaroo		pen		tomato
	bowl		elephant		key		pencil		train
	box		eraser		king		penguin		tree
	boys	**f**	farmer		kite		pig		turtle
	bus		fire		kiwi		pilot	**u**	unbrella
	button		firefighter		koala		plate		uniform
c	cage		flower	**l**	lemon		police officer	**v**	violin
	cake		fox		lion		pumpkin	**w**	wall
	car		frog	**m**	lunch	**q**	queen		watch
	cat	**g**	girls		map	**r**	rabbit		water
	chair		gorilla		mouse		ray		watermelon
	cow		grandmother	**n**	name		rocket		whale
	crab		grapes		net		room		window
	curry	**h**	hat		nurse	**s**	school	**y**	yo-yo
	curtains		helicopter	**o**	octopus		sea	**z**	zebra

Verb

c	catch
	close
	cook
	cut
d	drink
e	eat
g	go
o	open
p	pull
	push
r	run
s	sing
	sit
	sleep
	stand
	swim
t	throw
w	walk

Adjective

b	big
c	cold
f	full
l	long
h	hot
	hungry
s	short
	small

Preposition

in
on
under